Til Doubt Do Us Part

When changing beliefs change your marriage

BY
NAKEDPASTOR
DAVID HAYWARD

I dedicate this to my beautiful wife, Lisa. I love how your love and my love makes our love.

Copyright © 2020 David Hayward, nakedpastor

All rights reserved.

Introduction	1
Your Marriage And Your Crisis Of Faith	5
Can Your Marriage Survive Deconstruction?	9
Loving Them	13
Will Your Marriage Survive?	17
Changing Your Beliefs While Married	23
When You And Your Spouse No Longer Agree	25
Your Growth Must Lead To Your Freedom	29
When You're Not Given Space To Heal	33
Deconstruction, Marriage And Moral Confusion	37
Belief, Unbelief and Being In Love	43
Deconstruction And Marriage: You're Not A Robot!	47
Communication Is Key	51
The Dangers Of Deconstruction On Your Marriage	55
The Deconstruction Of Your Beliefs And Marriage	61
Being Different Is Good	65
Spiritual Transition And Marriage	69
Deconstruction, Demons, And Marriage	73
I Trust You With Your Spiritual Journey	75
Married But Questioning Your Beliefs	77
Married And Changing Your Beliefs	81
You And Your Spouse On Different Spiritual Paths	85
Deconstruction Is Not Betrayal	90
When You Break Your Partner's Heart	93
Your Whole Life Doesn't Have To Fall Apart	95
How To Change In Front Of Your Kids	97
Steps To Making New Friends For Your Marriage	103
When Your Marriage Doesn't Survive Deconstruction	107
Get Help For Your Marriage	111
The One Thing That Will Kill A Marriage	115

Staying In Love When You Don't Believe The Same 119
Deconstructing Spouses Of Ministry Spouses 123
Has The Church Come Between You? 127
Marriage, Deconstruction, and Having Fun 129
Loving Relationships And Changing Beliefs 133
10 Books For Committed Romantic Relationships 137
Conclusion 139

AKNOWLEDGMENTS

They say that it takes a village to raise a child. I think it also takes a village to raise a marriage. Lisa and I, as of this writing, have been married for forty years. We couldn't have done it without each other... which sounds funny but can't go without saying. Nor could we have done it without all the support we sought and utilized.

I want to thank my online community that is filled with a marvelous diversity of people. They let me test my books and courses on them. I appreciate their love and honesty. You're welcome to join if you want at TheLastingSupper.com.

My fans who follow nakedpastor are also an incredible collection of amazing people. I thank them for engaging with my posts and cartoons because they help me know what is helpful and what is not. I engage with them and hear from them every day, and I love every one of them.

Thanks to my editor, Amy Leibowitz Mitchell, who helps me sort my ideas and words so well. Thanks to my friend Jessi Blue Moxie for the great title idea. Also, I appreciate Eric Lawrence's eye for graphic design, the cover, and the assembly of the book.

I'm very grateful for Ron King and Thu Vo, good friends and also marriage therapists, who gave me wise and experienced feedback for this book.

Finally, Lisa. You are the most remarkable woman, and I'm lucky to be married to you. You are at least 50% responsible for the success of our marriage surviving our separate and joint deconstructions. I love you!

# INTRODUCTION

I had some friends read the manuscript of this book to make sure I wasn't missing anything. It had already gone through the capable hands of my editor. But I was looking more for content oversights.

One of them told me that the timeline seemed confusing to them. I mention Lisa and I throughout the chapters, but she wasn't sure when our trouble began, if it ended, and how our separate spiritualities played a role in it all.

So, here's a rough timeline to give you an idea of how things went for us.

Lisa and I were both very much on the same page when I was a pastor. We'd been working in the church for decades. But in 2009 I had a profound mystical experience where all my theological anguish evaporated. In a moment I saw that we are all one, that all that seems to separate us is thoughts and words, all of which are our attempts to apprehend and articulate a mystery that is greater than we can comprehend. I had immediate peace of mind that lasts to this day.

I was so profoundly changed by this experience that I began to share it on my nakedpastor blog.

This is when the real trouble began. Other churches, their pastors and members, as well as leaders in my denomination, began expressing concern. I knew my time was up.

Within a year, in early 2010, I left the ministry and the church. All with Lisa's total support.

Even though this mystical experience completed my long deconstruction, it began a new one. That is, my, and our, deconstruction from the church began.

At first it seemed easy, but after a while we realized we were in trouble. Mainly because I was not dealing with the new life well. We had basically been in the church and ministry our whole married lives and suddenly it was over. Lisa went to university to study nursing, and I taught English to international students preparing for their Masters in Business. This was a very different way of life than we were used to.

This adjustment that I unwrap for you in the following chapters was very difficult and treacherous. We almost didn't make it.

But after a couple of years of counseling, coaching, therapy, patience, and hope, our relationship endured.

Enter, the title, "Til Doubt Do Us Part". One reading of the title might suggest that when doubt enters your beliefs, the marriage will fall apart. But another reading might be that when doubt enters your beliefs, we are forced to individuate. That's what happened to Lisa and me. Necessarily! We were so entangled and entwined after years of working together in ministry and the church that we somehow lost our individual selves. It wasn't bad. We loved it. It worked at the time. But the time had come for us to become individuals, our own selves distinct from one another, and find our own paths. Fortunately, for us, this didn't mean separation. We found a way to not only make our marriage survive and work, but even improve!

It's 2020 when I write this, a decade later, and we're now better off than we've ever been. Lisa's a nurse, I'm busy with nakedpastor, our family is doing very well. You should detect from the following chapters roughly where we are in our spiritual lives.

Because I went through it myself, and because I see so many others going through it as well, I wanted to write it down and even create a course for couples struggling with the same thing.

It's a serious subject. I hope my cartoons lighten it up for you.

Also, please remember that these chapters first appeared as blog posts on nakedpastor. So there will be some repetition. Most of the chapters are short so I could post them to the many social media platforms I'm on.

I've put together a course along with a downloadable PDF workbook to follow this book. You can find it at davidhaywardcourses.com.

Finally, I've given a homework question at the end of each chapter. My suggestion is that you write it out in a letter to your partner for them to read, and hopefully they will write one to you too. Lisa and I found this practice very helpful in developing our communication skills in our marriage. Enjoy!

YOUR MARRIAGE AND YOUR CRISIS OF FAITH

For people who were really devout believers, deconstruction or going though a crisis of faith is global in its application.

I was just asking my wife, Lisa, about this. She is a nurse. I couldn't think of the right word to explain how deconstruction affects our lives globally. I asked her what word they use in treatment of a disease. She said "systemic": it's when we treat the whole body at once rather than just one aspect of the disease's manifestation.

Yes! That's exactly what it's like.

Because when we were those super-devout believers, our faith affected everything about our lives. Our beliefs weren't just isolated thoughts, but were systemic: the way we related with other people, the way we talked, the way we thought, the way we ate, the way we parented, the way we spent our spare time, the way we had sex, the way we spent our weekends, the way we thought about tragedy, the way we prepared for death, the way we thought about the future, the way we used our money, the way we thought about morality, the way we... well... the way we did everything.

Our devotion seeped into every little detail of our lives. When that belief system started to erode, it was like the glue that held our life together lost its grip and everything started to fall apart.

This is why deconstruction is not only an exciting time but a frightening and even dangerous one.

Exciting because we are growing deeper into our authenticity. Scary because we are losing the paradigm that made our lives meaningful. Dangerous because we are questioning the rules that kept our lives in check.

Lisa and I made it. Barely. But we made it. And we're better for it. We're more authentic. Our lives make sense in more mysterious ways. And we've navigated the dangerous waters to arrive in a peaceful and loving place. Everything's better!

The sweet, little Christian girl in the wedding photo behind them is gone. Forever. But a new person is on her way that will shine even brighter than before.

It's like gold. It looks dull at first. But fire exposes its essence and beauty.

Homework:

Describe in detail when and why you first fell in love with your partner.

CAN YOUR MARRIAGE SURVIVE DECONSTRUCTION?

When Lisa and I started deconstructing our faith and beliefs well into our marriage, we had no idea what to expect.

Our marriage almost didn't survive.

We had been madly in love for many years. We met in Bible College and served churches as a team for a long, long time. We were joined at the hip and were completely on the same page spiritually.

Then, deconstruction hit. Like a tsunami!

Suddenly, we had to figure out what it was that really brought us together and that really could keep us together.

Surely, it wasn't compatibility of beliefs! I didn't fall in love with her faith. I fell in love with her. And the same with her with me. If we were going to work this out and stay together, it could not mean one of us surrendering, compromising, and falling in line behind the other in terms of beliefs.

No! We came to the conclusion that it was love that drew us together and would keep us together. And with love comes mutual respect. And with mutual respect comes the desire to give space and allow others to be truly other in all their fascinating wonder.

So, we took some steps to make this happen. We talked to counselors and therapists and coaches. We read books. We talked... a lot. We made special dates. We fought and argued and split up for a night or two or three. But eventually we started to see light at the end of the long tunnel. It took a couple of years of rediscovering how to relate again, but we did it.

Lisa and I are very different. However, our love is the same, but stronger, more mature, wiser, and even sexier. We made it.

And if we can do it, so can you!

Homework:

What about your partner made you fall in love with them?

LOVING THEM

Love who people are and who they are becoming.

It didn't take long for Lisa and I to realize that we didn't marry stone statues.

We were both committed to growth. Our own and each other's.

We were young, passionate believers. But that wasn't the core of who we were.

I saw a glimpse of who Lisa was... a woman who at that time chose to be a passionate believer.

Same with me. Even though I chose at the time to be a passionate believer, the me who chose that was a person who made that choice.

Lisa's expression of herself felt harmonious with who she was. Same with me.

I didn't say "I do" to a Pentecostal woman, but to a woman who expressed herself as a Pentecostal woman. Her promise to me was to someone who chose to be Pentecostal then.

We took these expressions seriously and never predicted they'd change. We didn't marry the expression, but the one expressing.

See the difference? Because this is important.

When we went through our separate deconstructions, and because we respect how we each express ourselves, it was difficult to get beneath the expressions of who we were then. We were pastoring a church, were faithful church-goers and steadfast believers. But we had to rediscover that we weren't really those things. There was someone more essential making our choices.

Beneath our chaotic changes of expression were the David and the

Lisa who fell in love so many years ago.

We love them in their devotion and in their doubt. Because it's not their devotion or doubt we love, but them.

Homework:

Describe the essence of your partner. What are they deep down really like?

 WILL YOUR MARRIAGE SURVIVE?

I get messages from people all the time who are struggling in their marriages and relationships because they are deconstructing their beliefs. One thinks it's still okay to believe in God, and the other thinks it's stupid to believe in God. One still loves the faith, and the other hates Christians. So their relationship falls under strain, and they may end up separating and divorcing. This not only happens in marriage but in all our relationships.

But let's talk about our romantic relationships, and you can relate the same principles to any relationship.

When Lisa and I started deconstructing, our transition into a different kind of theology and spirituality was not only ground-shaking for us personally, but it put our relationship to an extreme test. There were times when we wondered if we would ever again be able to have a decent conversation without massive misunderstandings or that terrible tension we feel when we face an irreconcilable conflict.

But we did make it. Our relationship is healthier and happier than it's ever been before. Now when people ask me if it's possible for relationships to survive this, and if so how, here's the advice I give:

1. Don't be rash: When you were on the same page there was no need for patience. You had what you wanted: one hundred percent agreement. But as adults begin to grow, mature and change, disagreement is bound to and ought to occur. When one partner in a relationship changes, it forces the other to change. Marriage is like a crucible of transformation. We influence and change each other. This is what love does, actually. We make compromises (translate: improvements) in order to make our partner happy and our relationship more pleasant. So, when our partner starts to change, don't prematurely and immaturely dash out the door and abandon your partner or the relationship. Give

it time: they will change again and so may you!

2. Don't compromise too much: That is, if your partner can no longer tolerate you, gets impatient and angry with you and decides to leave, that's their problem, not yours. Their attempts to pressure you into a certain way of thinking is controlling and unfair. You didn't require that of them, and they shouldn't require it of you. The best and healthiest growth is natural and unforced. Everyone knows that. So don't compromise yourself too much by becoming what they demand you to be just so they'll be happy and stay with you. It's not worth it, because you are more important than the marriage. What I mean is, the healthiest relationship is between two consenting adults who don't manipulate or coerce one another. When you promised to take one another in sickness and in health, this meant spiritually too. So if they can't love you as you are right now, and as you are in your own spiritual process, then that's their problem, not yours. Don't sacrifice your essential self on the altar of their selfish insecurities and fears.

3. Understand true love: As adults mature, they begin to understand what true love is. When Lisa and I first met, she was the girl of my dreams. Literally, she "fit" into my fantasy of what the perfect woman was: she was beautiful and agreed with everything I believed. And I was the same for her. This is only natural. This is how young attraction works. Plus, unlike some relationships, Lisa and I were allowed to remain in that protective bubble for many, many years. It wasn't until we were in our forties where we started to deconstruct our beliefs and therefore gradually shift off the same page. We've aged, and we no longer believe identically. Sometimes we wonder if we're even in the same book or even library, never mind the same page! But we've learned an important lesson over the years. We actually have been changing all along, each of us in our own way, incrementally but surely. What enabled this to happen was our love for each other. We discovered that it wasn't sameness, agreement or compatibility that held us together but our love for one another. Those things might have brought us together, but they surely didn't keep us together. This is a very important lesson for lovers to learn as they mature.

4. Love is humility and respect. I was going to say love means tolerance, but tolerance has the ring of superiority to it... like, "I, because I am right and you are wrong, will tolerate you in your error until you finally see the light like I did and come around to my way of thinking!" I don't mean that. I mean love is humble and doesn't think of itself too highly. One should get to the point of realizing that life is full of mystery and that all knowledge and conclusions are transitory and provisional based on incoming research. Even scientists know this. But good lovers know this too. So they're humble about their beliefs and hold on to them loosely. One of the most delicious fruits of this is respect for others where they are. (Unless their beliefs lead them to violent acts against others.) So in loving relationships, there is mutual respect that goes deeper than held beliefs. That is, we trust our loved one to take care of themselves intellectually and spiritually. The beliefs are just thoughts rippling on the surface of a deeper reality called the self, and we trust their self to their own search and discoveries. I do not agree with everything Lisa believes, but I do agree that she has the right to her own journey her own way, and I trust her with that. We can observe each other with delight as we discover how best to find our truth and live it in our own personal lives.

5. Final advice: Live happy now! For me, it means getting fresh flowers and treats for Lisa even in the midst of apparent disagreement. It means going for walks together and going out on dates. It means sitting down and intentionally having a difficult conversation. It means enjoying sex... where theology isn't invited. We hear weird stories, but seriously, the quality of sex should not depend on your beliefs, so I take this is a metaphor for relationships generally. I remember once when we were driving and Lisa asked what I did about prayer now. My first reaction was defensiveness and feeling perturbed. But I took a deep breath and began trying to articulate what I thought about it. What helped was even though she cared what I thought about prayer, I also knew my ideas weren't going to kill our marriage. She wasn't going to judge me on a pass/fail model and kick me out of the car if I was wrong. So I took advantage of this opportunity, and it actually helped me understand myself and my thoughts about prayer a little better. Plus, she's just a good

listener. It's true, for me, that speaking and writing helps me not only articulate my own position but understand it better. What I'm saying in all this is that even though we go through times of strain in our marriage because of deconstruction, we behave as though it is transitory, a passing storm, and that we will weather it and come out of the other side better and stronger.

Look, I know of many couples who just couldn't make it through their deconstruction together. Many people realize in this season that they really don't love their partner anymore and are very unhappy, and they decide to separate and eventually divorce. That's okay. It happens a lot because for the first time in their spiritual lives they may feel like they finally have permission to be honest about the actual state of their union.

But if you do still love the one you're with, if you do still love the person you married, then you can work it out. I've done it, and I've seen others do it. It doesn't mean you'll necessarily and eventually come to a place of perfect agreement again, but it can mean you will come to a deeper place of love for one another as each of you are. Your love will stretch and therefore grow to include everything about your partner... even the parts you didn't expect or sign up for. That's what love does. Even romantic love.

It's not always a pleasant process. Who said love was easy? But it is always worth it.

Homework:

How do you feel controlled by your partner that limits your freedom?

CHANGING YOUR BELIEFS WHILE MARRIED

Do you want to know the biggest reason people want to talk with me?

I'll tell you: one or both are deconstructing their beliefs and it's affecting their marriage.

I know all about it. Lisa and I got married when she was 19 and I was 21. We met in Bible College. We were on the same page spiritually for decades. Then deconstruction set in, and everything changed. Our compatible beliefs were among the top ingredients in the glue that kept us together. When we ran out of that, we had to figure out, and fast, what would truly keep us together.

We discovered it is love. True love. Love that respects and honors the other person in all their singular uniqueness.

Now, our relationship is better than it has ever been. We've been together for almost 40 years! We're actually thankful we went through that crisis in our relationship because it forced us to tap into a deeper love. And deeper's better!

Homework:

What is one terrible time that your relationship survived? Why did it?

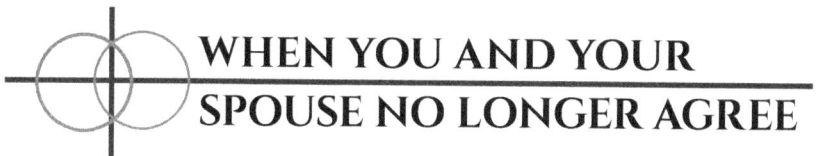

WHEN YOU AND YOUR SPOUSE NO LONGER AGREE

What do you do when you and your partner no longer agree?

I know all about it. Lisa and I were there. Still are!

For years, even decades, we were pretty much on the same page. Then, as deconstruction set in and our beliefs and theology began to undergo a dramatic and traumatic shift, we drifted apart.

We used to be so much on the same page we were indiscernible. There was never any thought about feeling different. There was no concern about arguing things through to an agreeable position. There was never the effort to compromise our beliefs or values.

It really hit us when we left the ministry and the church in 2010. It was then we realized we were no longer on the same page, maybe not even in the same book, maybe not even in the same library!

Sometimes it felt like she went her way, and I went mine. She went to get her nursing degree, and I went to teach at a university. We used to share the same beliefs, spirituality and church life. We were joined at the hip. Then we weren't. It felt strange and scary! There were times we didn't think we were going to make it.

We got help. We learned how to renegotiate. We wondered if maybe this was a good thing. Perhaps before, we were so enmeshed that we weren't really individuals. Maybe before, even though we were very happy, we were kind of codependent on one another and lacked a healthy autonomy. I don't know. It worked for us then, but it no longer did now.

Good news: we made it! We're good. Really good. Better than ever!

What did it take?

Help in the form of therapists, counselors, coaches. Patience because we still hoped we loved each other and this would work itself out. Wisdom to realize that love keeps us together, not compatibility. Humility to embrace the other in all their profound complexity. And love, the glue that joined us together so many years ago and keeps us together still.

We've been married almost 40 years, and the romance is still alive! Even though we are on different pages theologically and spiritually, love is what keeps us together.

This is totally possible for you too!

I want to add something here: sometimes, when deconstruction hits you and you change your beliefs, you might realize that you were never really in love in the first place or that your love has died or that the pressure and expectations of your church forced you to marry and stay together even though it wasn't right. The veil has been lifted, and you see your marriage for what it is, and it might be better to go your separate ways. Understood!

But… if you suspect you're still in love, even if everything seems a mess, I think your marriage can make it! I talk with people all the time in this situation, and my own experience along with my observations of other relationships convinces me that almost any marriage can be saved!

Homework:

What is your biggest disagreement with your spouse and why does it upset you?

YOUR GROWTH MUST LEAD TO YOUR FREEDOM

Probably the best book on marriage is David Schnarch's, "Passionate Marriage" (a must read). Here's just one quote:

"Crucibles are always interlocking. When one partner goes into his crucible, the other partner goes into hers— or gets out of the marriage."

What this means... and I've seen it over and over again... is that if one person commits to their own personal growth and change, the other partner must enter into their own commitment to growth and change. If the partner doesn't, it inevitably leads to an often irreparable widening of the gap between them. This leads to an emotional separation that will finally manifest in a physical one.

I apply this to any relationship, including yours with the church. Your life task, if you choose to accept it, is to be committed to your own growth and freedom. If your relationship with the church is increasingly strained because of its unwillingness to embrace and make room for your growth, then separation will occur.

The separation will begin inwardly at first. But eventually, if you have an ounce of conviction and a dash of courage, it will begin to manifest outwardly as well.

You must be free, and if your church doesn't allow it, I recommend separation.

Walk away!

However, be warned! Freedom, I have discovered, is a beautiful but terrible thing.

As Carl Jung said:

"To become acquainted with oneself is a terrible shock. It's hard admitting that our lives are full of error and self-deception. But this very admission, though painful, makes possible its opposite— a differentiated life, lived with integrity. Tears of recognition and relief often flow with the dawn of self-awareness. But while the truth will set you free, remember the psychologist Erich Fromm's observation of humankind's attempt to escape from such freedom. The truth is liberating— but only when you have the courage to live it."

Although your freedom is urgent and necessary. don't take it lightly.

Perhaps you know an ex-convict... someone who has lived many years in prison. At least you've seen one in a movie or read about one in a book. Their transition into the real world is traumatic and sometimes impossible. This is why there are organizations that assist these people and help them integrate into life on the outside.

So your fight for your own personal freedom is twofold:

You have to fight to get it.

You have to fight to keep it.

But it is always worth it.

Homework:

What is one way you would like to personally exercise your freedom?

WHEN YOU'RE NOT GIVEN SPACE TO HEAL

I awakened very early this morning from a dream. When I wake up I usually can't get back to sleep, so I got up and made coffee. I'm drinking it now and decided to write my weekly letter to you. It's been percolating for a while, and it's time I wrote it.

(About dreams: I have an online course to help people interpret their own dreams.)

But what I really want to talk to you about it is community... particularly how I believe community needs, in order to be valuable, to be able to provide space and time for people to heal themselves.

Just a few days ago a friend of mine was kicked out of a group because she's going through a divorce and the leader was uncomfortable with her anger. My friend gave me permission to share the letter she received:

"I am afraid I have some bad news. I have to discontinue your blog posts on (our) page.

"As much as I understand the pain of your marriage, I have been watching your progression into bitterness and even worldliness over the past several months. It has come to open slander against your former church and I can't abide in that.

"I am urging you to deal with this sinful anger and bitterness that I can see (from hundreds of miles away) before it ruins your life. I am urging you to stop making such postings about your personal life on facebook and in your personal blog, they do not reflect well on your Christian testimony.

"I will be praying for you."

Typical! I say typical because this is what happens almost all the time. I ranted about this in a video on Facebook. It's getting more attention than I thought it would.

So I had a dream the night this happened to my friend and she shared her story with me. Let me share with you my dream:

"I am in an old house with many people, friends and old friends, who are still very much believers and church-goers. I can tell something's wrong. I can tell they have an issue with me. So I press them. Finally, one of them blurts out, "We're tired of your negativity! It's having an effect on us, and even on our children!" I am very hurt and upset by this. They fail to understand the seriousness and the implications and ramifications of what I've gone through and what other people I know are going through. I feel an implicit pressure to return to the fold, but I realize this would be at great cost to my conscience, integrity, and honesty. I would have to live a lie. I'm sad this means they will remain angry with me."

So obviously what happened to my friend really resonated with me more than I was conscious of. But more than resonated! I realized after I had this dream that I responded so strongly to what happened to her because it represents exactly what happened to me and to people I love.

People, and our communities, can handle struggle... up to a point. I don't know exactly where the line is. It depends on the severity of what happened to the struggler and the grace-quotient of the people. For minor things, maybe a month or two. For bigger things, maybe a few months or a little more. Then it's time to get over it and move on and stop being a drag on the rest of us!

This is one of the main reasons why I launched The Lasting Supper. It was to provide a space for people to be very real for as long as required. Why? Because I've seen in my own life and in the lives of many others that when we are given space and time and support, we learn to help ourselves and heal ourselves. Even from major traumas!

So let's keep on being real and being healers. Process for as long as it takes.

Help yourself! We can do this!

Homework:

What is one area of your life you feel you need to be given space to heal?

DECONSTRUCTION, MARRIAGE AND MORAL CONFUSION

One of the things I experienced when I left the church was moral confusion.

I think this is something to be expected during the deconstruction of our religion, beliefs or faith.

Like I've said before, for the first year after leaving the ministry and the church I was numb. Frozen. I thought I was doing great, but looking back I obviously wasn't.

Then, as I thawed over the next two years, this became a time of very intense moral confusion. I drank more than usual, wanted to smoke and sometimes did, thought about trying pot but didn't, increased my swearing vocabulary and frequency of use, dared to get really angry at people and tell them exactly what I thought, and outright avoided people in the grocery store or whatever.

Ya! I know. Small potatoes. These things are meaningless to me now. Not at the time though.

So here are some big potatoes. I'm going to be as candid as I dare. I also got very confused about my marriage and family and home and even myself. I felt trapped and I wanted to cast off all restraint. All of it! I'm not joking– this was one of the most traumatic times in my life, in our marriage, for my family (because my kids knew what was going on) and the few friends we had left. I couldn't understand this strange and unfamiliar powerful drive within me that just wanted to run away from everything! I wanted out! Out of every responsibility. Every commitment. Every union.

Every expectation. Even my own personality. Everything! I didn't care! Even when Lisa was crying, I felt nothing. Even when she left those few times, I felt nothing. When I think back to the pain I was in and the pain I caused I still get very emotional about it.

You know what this sounds like, right? Adolescence. In many ways many of us are unprepared for the real world. It's not our fault. We just haven't been given the proper tools to grow up yet.

There are stages of moral development. I haven't looked these up.

These are mine:

1. infantile: fear of punishment
2. childish: fear of rejection
3. adolescent: fear of limitations
4. adult: fear of betraying our conscience
5. mature adult: fear of harming humanity

"Fear" isn't the best word, especially as we mature, but you get the point. Also, at some point the law, which is external to us as infants and children, endeavors to become internal as we mature so that it becomes a part of our own moral fiber. We develop moral integrity and a mature conscience.

We aren't good because we must but because we desire it.

I think the church is excellent at fostering infantile and childish stages of moral development. But, and I speak generally, it sucks at helping us break free of the external law to learn how to internalize what is right and good and integrate this with our consciences.

Now, some people mosey along with no spikes in aberrant behavior. They just gently develop like the unfolding of a rose in the morning dew of a sunrise.

Not me. And not like some of you. I've always had to test my boundaries.

Like an emotionally adolescent kid going off to college, I employed the good old pendulum swing. You too? We act out. We experiment. We go overboard. We break all the rules that restricted us before. We alarm not only those around us, but even ourselves. We can actually become reckless and careless and hurt others. And if you're anything like me, there's something about all this that makes you just not care.

Lisa and I talked about this quite a bit because she experienced this phenomena in her own way as well. We concluded that this happens because:

1. We were never taught to become morally independent.
2. We left the policing church community.
3. No one was watching.
4. There were no ramifications to our actions.

Basically, when we left the church and that whole culture, there was no one watching how we lived, and there would be no serious consequences to our actions, such as shaming, shunning, excommunication, or my losing my job as a pastor. That was all behind us.

It was a strange and scary feeling, realizing that I could, say, leave Lisa, and no one in my new world would even bat an eye.

It took a couple of years, but finally that which was morally important to me percolated down into my deepest self. What I valued most became internalized and eventually integrated itself with my inner life. And just in the nick of time.

There were plenty of people telling me to "follow your heart" or "do what you want to do right now" or "just do what makes you happy"! I'm not sure why, but I didn't follow their advice. I can't say it was because I was strong.

Maybe I was afraid. Or maybe something held me back. I just don't know. I salute Lisa's grace, patience, courage and candor with me. That is the first ingredient. I also thank my counselor, who dragged me through brutal sessions of painful honesty. That's the second ingredient. But why I didn't trash everything I now value more than ever, I'm not entirely sure. That's the secret recipe I haven't figured out yet. I'm grateful though.

Also, you may come out the other side with a different morality than when you went in. It is quite amazing what the lack of community policing, monitoring and control can do to the liberated individual.

- Maybe I'm giving you the heads up that this might happen to you.
- Or maybe I've explained what has happened to you.
- Or maybe this is a promise that if you somehow find it in you to hold on, what you value most will integrate with who you truly are.

Peace on your path, my friends!

Homework:

Are you feeling tempted to break the rules in your relationship? How?

© nakedpastor.com
D.Hayward
SO MOM AND DAD I'VE FALLEN IN LOVE WITH A GUY I WANT YOU TO MEET BUT I WANT YOU TO KNOW AHEAD OF TIME THAT HE DOESN'T GO TO CHURCH OR BELIEVE THE SAME AS I DO.

BELIEF, UNBELIEF AND BEING IN LOVE

The father of one of my first girlfriends wanted to meet me in order to pass a test.

He asked me to look at the wallpaper on their dining room wall and tell me what I saw.

I saw nothing but wallpaper.

I failed the test.

He said that there were faces of demons in design of the wallpaper, and the fact that I couldn't see them was proof that I was demon-possessed.

He pronounced that I had a "pharisaical spirit" and couldn't date his daughter.

I often talk with people who are terrified because someone they love doesn't believe the same way they do or doesn't believe at all.

They are afraid that they are:

1. disobeying God by unequally yoking them to an unbeliever
2. blinded by love and making a foolish decision they will regret
3. stepping into the trap of a terrible relationship

My strategy is to encourage them:

1. If there is a God (not all of them are sure), then this God should be loving, gracious, and caring, and desire your genuine happiness.
2. Love is wonderful and, if you find it, enjoy it. Love not only covers a multitude of sins, but is the essential glue of a healthy relationship... not compatible beliefs!

3. I know many healthy relationships where they differ in their beliefs. In fact, Lisa and I started out on the same page and now are on very different pages. We've discovered, like so many couples, that having space for others in all their diversity makes for an extremely rich, satisfying, exciting, and long-lasting relationship.

Don't let the narrow-mindedness and fears of others rob you of love.

Homework:

What's something your partner believes that you don't or doesn't believe that you do? Do you respect them anyway?

DECONSTRUCTION AND MARRIAGE: YOU'RE NOT A ROBOT!

When people ask how our marriage survived deconstruction, I've said communication. But maybe it's the capacity to accept change.

When Lisa and I first fell in love, I wonder what would have happened if she said, "I love you, but I need to know you're okay if I change, because I'm going to since I plan on growing!"

My first thought would have been, "As long as you don't stop loving me. I don't ever want to lose you!"

That's fear! The fear of loss. The only way to prevent loss is to prevent change. If nothing changes then everything stays the same... two kids madly in love fulfilling each others' fantasies forever.

We form fantasies of our partners... what they look like, how they behave, how they love us. When they fulfill our fantasies, everything's perfect. As soon as they deviate from it, the real work begins.

The sufferings in our relationships are rooted in fantasy. Disappointment is the failure of reality to correspond to our fantasy.

What if we accepted our partner as they are rather than as we wish them to be?

In some ways Lisa's a different person. But not essentially. Deep within her is the desire to grow. To change! She has and will. Me too!

Embedded in most marriage vows is the acknowledgment that things change, so we promise our love will remain constant throughout these changes.

If you are deconstructing your beliefs and faith, hopefully you've already agreed that change is inevitable, that often it's not what we wished, and that we will honor the change our partner undergoes and expect the same from them.

Change happens. But love can too!

Deconstruction takes more than an hour.

Sometimes our partners don't understand that.

When we experience the deconstruction of our beliefs, often our loved ones can't comprehend what's happening.

We don't either! And that's part of the problem.

Even though both Lisa and I deconstructed, it was at different times, at different speeds and with different manifestations.

For most of us, deconstruction is an involuntary process. We didn't ask for it. It happened to us!

However, I do believe that those who deconstruct are by default committed to personal growth, so in a sense they invited the deconstruction of their beliefs.

Yes, deconstruction equals growth!

But we had no idea what it would feel like!

One of the most impossible things to do during your deconstruction is for you to explain yourself.

When your beliefs crumble, you must learn a new way of thinking and therefore a new way of speaking.

The old thoughts with their attending words no longer suffice. You're looking for new ones.

This is why it's so difficult to comprehend and articulate the process while you're in it.

Your partner might believe you've lost control, that you're being lazy, non-committal, and backsliding, or just being a jerk.

The truth more likely is that you are the victim of a profound but painful growth process, and it might be a while before you find your footing again.

It isn't helpful to say, "Please stop this!" That's asking you to stop growing.

You'd rather hear, "Hey, you're growing. Take as long as you need. I'm here for you."

They might even say, "I hope you're not contagious because I don't want what you got!"

Homework:

What is the biggest change you've seen in your partner? Have you given them space for that? How about yourself? Have you been given space for change?

HOW AM I GOING TO TELL MY WIFE I DON'T BELIEVE ALL THIS ANYMORE?
HOW AM I GOING TO TELL MY PARENTS I DON'T BELIEVE ALL THIS ANYMORE?
HOW AM I GOING TO TELL MY HUSBAND I DON'T BELIEVE ALL THIS ANYMORE?
Hayward
© nakedpastor.com

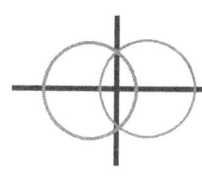

COMMUNICATION IS KEY

Here we see a family going through deconstruction.

Each one alone.

Why not do it together?

For example, with your spouse:

I keep saying communication is key. Communication is critical. Communication is the cure.

Here's some advice about communicating about your deconstruction with your loved ones:

1. Arrange a time.

2. Promise you'll try to not get defensive. Just speak descriptively.

3. Promise you'll try to not get judgmental. Just listen without evaluating.

4. Have drinks while you talk (Lisa and I have "scotch and Bailey's nights").

5. Settle in for a long talk.

6. If you have trouble articulating where you are, just try.

7. Determine to be honest. Share your emotions, not just your thoughts.

8. Don't be insecure. Pretend you're not emotionally invested in the other.

9. Trust the other is on their journey not by accident but by choice.

10. Realize it's not going to get settled today. This is a process.

I want to share something with you:

Honesty is sexy. Connecting through honest communication can be very alluring. Finding compatibility at a deeper level can be very sensual. Discovering new facets of your spouse can be very romantic.

Who knows where this could lead?

For Lisa and me, it lead to a reboot for our marriage and our relationship's better than it's ever been.

Give it a shot!

Homework:

Set up a date where you can talk honestly for a couple of hours. Snacks. Wine. Music. Candles. Kids asleep or babysat. Talk about what you're going through without judging, correcting, or interrupting. If conversation is too volatile, write each other a letter and read them to each other without any interruptions, corrections, or rebuttals.

I'M SORRY. HE CAN'T COME TO THE PHONE RIGHT NOW. HE'S LOSING HIS RELIGION.
@nakedpastor.com

THE DANGERS OF DECONSTRUCTION ON YOUR MARRIAGE

Deconstruction... the changing of your beliefs, the crumbling of your faith, the loss of your religion... can be a dangerous process. It isn't for all, but I think it is for most.

This is a letter I wrote to the members of The Lasting Supper, my online community where we help and support each other deconstruct and reconstruct our spiritual autonomy and independence in healthy ways.

What I want to write about today in my weekly letter to you is a kind of a warning. I want to warn you about the dangers of deconstruction.

I've been through it. When I left the ministry and the church five years ago, I had no idea what devastation I was about to undergo.

Deconstruction = Devastation.

There's no other way of looking at it. Sorry. It's for the good, but getting there can be rough.

I suppose there are some people who experience a very smooth and serene transition in the deconstruction of their faith and beliefs. But in my observation they're rare.

The norm is rocky and stormy.

So I will share with you a few of the dynamics I personally experienced, and still do to some extent.

1. DEPRESSION:

The first thing I want to warn you about is depression. For the first year after I left the church I thought I was okay. In fact, I thought I was really happy. I felt free for the first time since I could remember. But... and my good wife Lisa pointed this out to me after about a year... I was depressed. I wasn't feeling anything because I was actually numb. Emotionally, I was frozen.

The nasty thing about depression is that it isn't contained. It doesn't restrict itself to one little corner of your brain. It's like campfire smoke that permeates all it touches. It gets into everything and clings to it. No matter what you use to get it out, it still lingers.

This is what happens to anyone who experiences any kind of trauma. We lock down as a coping mechanism. It is human, natural and often healthy because it can protect us from something more serious. Freezing emotionally enables us to let the trauma melt in increments and slowly evaporate rather than melting all at once and drowning us in a flood of despair forever.

The best thing to do is recognize it. "I'm depressed. I'm in a slump. Emotionally, I am frozen." Just admitting it is the first huge step. Recognize it. Acknowledge it. Embrace it.

Now that you've done that, you can take very certain steps to address it. It took me some good counseling, coaching and spiritual direction to guide me out of that slump. And the gentle patience of my wife, kids and friends.

In other words, get help! It's just for a season, but you can make sure you weather it well.

2. CONFUSION:

The next thing I would like to warn you about is confusion. When I left the church the confusion that wrapped itself around my brain was debilitating. Theologically and philosophically, I had come to a place of peace of mind that has never left and is now, I believe, a permanent state I enjoy. But, on the other hand, I couldn't see the road ahead at all. I was completely blind and in the dark. I'd always had a sense of purpose and destiny that was now gone. What's next? I had no idea. This was an uncomfortably new experience for me.

But I recognized this from times it had happened before. I've personally tested this and now I know it is true: when you let a question abide in your mind, in time the solution will come. You can read more about this in my book, "Questions are the Answer" (on Amazon). I purposely didn't say "the answer will come" because it often isn't like an answer to a math problem. It has happened to me so many times and proven itself to me over and over again that when a deep question of profound importance troubles my intellect, I will just let it stay there and do its work. Over time, a peace will come that will resolve the tension in your mind. It might take days, weeks, months or years. But it will come. Promise!

Learning to live with the question is a skill you probably were not taught in the church. But it is a skill you must learn. This does not mean you give up. This does not mean you reject the question. This does not mean you cease your studies. This means you trust the question to unlock itself and reveal the deeper truth you are seeking when the time is ripe.

Seek and you will find. Wisdom is the reward of the patiently seeking.

3. STRAIN:

The third and final dynamic I want to warn you about is the strain deconstruction will put on your personal life. Especially on your relationships. Especially on your marriage. I saw it in my own life, and I see it all the time in the lives of others.

No matter how young or old you are, it's like a kind of mid-life crisis happens. Indeed, I claim that deconstruction looks very much like a mid-life crisis. It is a crisis. And it drops right in the middle of your life. Hence... mid-life crisis!

For now let me say this: the worst time to make big life decisions and changes is in the middle of a crisis. Endure the strain and wait.

I remember the overwhelming feeling I had at the end of my time in the church was feeling trapped. Then in one evening it became clear that my escape was laid out before me, and I should take it. I did, and the freedom I felt was amazing. But this feeling of being trapped infiltrated everything else in my life, including my religion, my home, my work with nakedpastor, my marriage, and my family and friends. I wanted to run away from everything. Including nakedpastor! Lisa's always been great. There was nothing wrong there, but my attitude betrayed that I didn't want the feeling of being trapped in anything, and my confused mind translated this into the idea that I didn't want anymore commitments and that I wanted to run free and alone for the rest of my days. No, I didn't run off with another woman. I just wanted out of everything! But I imagined myself a grumpy old fart alone in a one-bedroom apartment hanging over a stove with a cigarette hanging out of his mouth, a tumbler of scotch in one hand and a stirring spoon in the other, making Kraft Dinner. A nightmare! But at the time, it felt better than being trapped. Crazy! I know.

I'm so glad I didn't act on this. Whew! Sooooo glad. But I confess to you that I dragged Lisa and my kids through my own personal Hell and made it theirs for a while as well. Rather than taking some advice from people, like, "Do what will make you happy right now!" I took what ended up being saner and wiser advice, like, "Wait until the crisis is over and decide then. You're not in a healthy enough space to make a wise choice." I did wait. And am I ever happy I did. What devastation I would have caused!

This is not to say that your marriage or relationships won't suffer or that they don't need to end or change. That's not what I'm saying. The strain will either expose the faults that are in your relationship, or it might create new ones, or it will attempt to. I just want to warn you that during your deconstruction the strain on your relationships and your marriage will be real and threatening.

So go in with your eyes open!

Depression, confusion and strain. Not happy words. But real ones that describe a reality. My promise is that if you endure these unhappy realities, that happier ones will result. Some of the ugliest seeds produce the most beautiful flowers.

Homework:

What scares you the most about what you and your partner are going through?

THIS DECONSTRUCTION I'M GOING THROUGH... IT'S ONE THING TO LET GO OF CERTAIN BELIEFS. THEY'RE JUST THOUGHTS! THAT'S HARD ENOUGH. BUT WHAT DO I DO WITH THE INTENSE SPIRITUAL EXPERIENCES I HAD AND THE POWERFUL EMOTIONS I REALLY FELT THAT WERE CONNECTED TO THOSE BELIEFS?! I CAN'T DENY THEY WERE REAL. THAT'S WHAT'S REALLY MESSING ME UP!
D. Hayward
©nakedpastor.com

THE DECONSTRUCTION OF YOUR BELIEFS AND MARRIAGE

One of the most difficult challenges I ever undertook was to deconstruct my beliefs and stay married.

Honestly, there were many times Lisa and I didn't think we were going to make it. But we did. And I'm so grateful.

(DISCLAIMER: Some couples I've known, when one or the other enter into deconstruction, they sometimes discover they were never really in love, got married under naive or inappropriate conditions, or that they have fallen out of love and into a rut. Divorce becomes a viable option for many marriages in these cases.)

However, there are many marriages that should remain. There are many people who should work hard to keep their relationship intact. Yes, you will experience traumatic and cataclysmic change, but if you do a few things right, there's a very good chance that you will make it and that your marriage will not only survive but get better.

Like I said, Lisa and I made it. Our marriage is better than ever. But we did a few things that helped us survive.

1. We talked. Communication is key! Process everything.

2. We got help. Counselors, therapists, coaches. You name it. Do it.

3. We read good books on marriage.

4. We didn't make decisions under confusion. Wait for clarity!

5. We learned love kept us together, not compatibility. Respect their uniqueness.

6. We kept romance alive even when the fire wasn't there. Date. Buy flowers. Talk.

7. We remembered what drew us together and how madly in love we were. Remember?

8. We embraced change as not only inevitable but preferable. Welcome change!

9. We held out in hopes that things would get better. Hope!

10. We hung out with other healthy couples. Find supportive friends who model love.

I could go on. But these are the keys to helping your marriage survive deconstruction.

Remember, you used to be so much on the same page spiritually. Now, you're not! You have to learn how to love at a deeper level than compatibility. You will each grow in different ways at different paces. Respect and honor that.

As one stretches in a more liberal direction while the other stretches in a more conservative one, this will put new strains on your marriage. But if you learn to work with the bonds of marriage as if they're elastics instead of chains, you will succeed.

For Lisa and I, the rough patch was for about 2 years. That sounds like a long time. But it was worth it, and the work paid off. Now our marriage is stronger and more delightful than ever!

Homework:

What do you want your relationship to look like?

LET'S JUST BE QUIET UNTIL WE CAN TALK ABOUT SOMETHING WE CAN AGREE ON!
FINE!
NICE COFFEE, HUH?
©nakedpastor.com

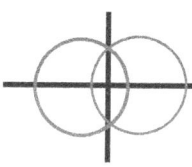

BEING DIFFERENT IS GOOD

Diversity is the demonstration of love.

I will share a little about Lisa's and my journey together.

When we first met and for the first few decades of our marriage we were very much on the same page. You could call us an homogenous unit. We were deeply in love, and our spiritual compatibility was never questioned. In fact, it was safely assumed. Our spiritual and religious life together was easy.

Then, when the deconstruction of our beliefs set in, we found ourselves drifting away from our spiritual center onto our own unique spiritualities with their differing beliefs.

This was a traumatic experience for us.

There were times we weren't sure we were going to make it together. It was terrifying. We used to be so on the same page. Now we weren't sure we were even in the same book!

Normally what is done is, first, one and the other attempts to bring the other in alignment with his or her beliefs.

Second, when each of us is cautious about sacrificing our own journey for the sake of the other and the relationship, we humbly attempt to modify our own positions as a kind of compromise, hoping we can meet in an imaginary middle.

Third, when the previous strategies fail, we may come to the conclusion that saving the relationship is impossible because the chasm between us is too great.

Fourth, having survived the previous failed attempts at reconciliation and not desiring to separate, we may begin to learn to respect and even honor the chosen path of our partner.

The fourth way is the best.

It's best because I believe it is the highest demonstration of love. It isn't love to force another to your position. It isn't love to feel forced to sacrifice yours. It isn't love to reject the other. (Although sometimes love is acknowledging incompatible differences and letting the other go.)

It is love to honor diversity in the relationship.

Lisa and I have discovered that unity does not necessarily mean homogeneity. We've also learned that love does not mean spiritual compatibility. We experience love in our diversity at a deeper level than we've ever loved before.

Loving a mirror reflection of ourselves is hardly a challenge. But loving the other as other is the true test of love because we've come to know that the expression of unity is the dynamic union of diversity. Our love has deepened.

This does not mean our challenges have ceased. Rather, we must daily commit to love in all our difference and diversity. It's a new and exciting way to be in relationship.

The same dynamic can be applied to the church. What happens between Lisa and I can happen in larger communities as well. I've experienced it, the deep appreciation of the expression of an inherent unity that underlies the vast diversity expressed within the community. Whether it is diversity in gender, sexuality, lifestyle, economics, race, age, ability, or beliefs, these are, when given space, all manifestations of the deep and underlying unity and reconciliation of all things, and are appreciated as such. We appreciate that differences are not anomalies to unity, but manifestations of it.

Churches nor members should force others to conform to their beliefs. Neither should both endeavor to find the impossible and imaginary middle ground of mutual compromise. What we often see instead is a separation into differing tribes.

Rather, why not embrace the wide diversity representative of the whole human race and enjoy the truest demonstration of unity with mutual respect and love? As we mature, we realize that homogeneity is not unity but uniformity.

True unity is diversity conjoined in love.

This makes a good marriage!

Homework:

What about your partner is really different than you but that you've always appreciated.

I WONDER WHAT THE MINISTER AND EVERYONE WILL THINK IF WE INCLUDE IN OUR VOWS, "I PROMISE TO LOVE YOU EVEN IF YOU CHANGE YOUR BELIEFS."
Hayward
@nakedpastor

SPIRITUAL TRANSITION AND MARRIAGE

Lisa and I have been a long and incredible journey, and I love where we are.

I have been thinking a lot today about spiritual transition and marriage. I was talking with someone recently who said that when one of the partners in a marriage goes through profound spiritual upheaval and transition, their marriage almost always ends up in the garbage. That's what he said. I agree. That's what I've witnessed as well.

Lisa and I have gone through some pretty scary spiritual transitions throughout our marriage, but none as profound, cataclysmic or traumatic as the past two years. Well, when you get right down to it, the last 6 months. Let me be honest: there were days I did not think, nor did she, that we were going to make it. But we did. So far. We're stronger for it. And that's all we can ask for.

What has kept us together? It certainly has not been theological agreement. It has not been spiritual compatibility. It has not been authority and submission or adherence to basic fundamental beliefs. We do not even believe it has been divine intervention.

I'll tell you what I think it is that kept us together: love! And this is what our love looks like: we affirm an individual's right, responsibility and privilege to search for, find and walk their own spiritual path. I love Lisa. She loves David. Whatever path she is on or I am on is not her or me. It is just our respective paths. I am one of the most confused people on the planet. But I admit it. And she knows it. However, she loves me in spite of it and affirms my search. Because when the sun sets, it is still David lying next to her, loving her and believing in her and appreciating her beauty, inside and out.

This applies to church, to religious community. This is how we practiced being pastors of our churches. We affirmed the spiritual walk of others. We loved the person, affirmed their search and edified their paths. This is how relationship works. This is how our inherent unity is manifested.

It is not from agreement, similarity or compatibility, but from an affirming, inclusive love.

Homework:

What are some new differences in your partner that you don't like? Can you adjust or do you feel your partner needs to?

WHAT'S REALLY HAPPENING
I'M JUST QUESTIONING ALL MY BELIEFS. I MEAN, I HAVE A LOT OF DOUBTS AND I'M FINDING IT VERY DIFFICULT AND SCARY.
WHAT HE THINKS IS HAPPENING
HI STEVE. I'M A DEMON THAT'S TAKEN OVER YOUR WIFE. SHE'S LOST FOREVER. LET HER GO. YOU'RE NEXT!
Hayward
© nakedpastor.com

DECONSTRUCTION, DEMONS, AND MARRIAGE

I hear from people all the time who are struggling in their marriage because one or both are deconstructing their beliefs or their faith or their relationship to the church or all the above.

Plain and simple: talk it through.

NOTHING beats conversation!

This woman is trying to talk openly, honestly and vulnerably about her spiritual journey.

Her husband can't get out of his worldview. He's stuck in his beliefs and wishes she would stay stuck in hers.

I'm not sure they're going to make it.

But they might.

Indeed, they can!

Homework:

Is there anything about your partner that feels really foreign to who you thought they were? Explain.

HEY! WHAT IF I'M NOT BACKSLIDING? WHAT IF I'M ACTUALLY GROWING?!
©nakedpastor.com

I TRUST YOU WITH YOUR SPIRITUAL JOURNEY

Lisa and I have been married a long time.

It took us a while to learn a very important lesson:

She needs to trust me with my own spiritual journey.

I need to trust her with hers.

This is the only way a healthy marriage can work.

If you're going through deconstruction (changing your beliefs, etcetera), both of you have to give space to the other out of respect for their ability to find their own way.

If you are on different pages... say, one is more conservative and the other more liberal... all you can do is trust them with that choice.

Otherwise, you end up either judging or disdaining one another.

Do you know what I think the number one killer of a marriage is?

Contempt.

Don't go there. Work it out. Figure out how to restore and maintain respect for and trust in one another.

Because if change is a given, then trust is a must.

Homework:

Where do you feel you need to relinquish control and respect your partner's choices?

MARRIED BUT QUESTIONING YOUR BELIEFS

Relationships in general and marriages in particular struggle to survive deconstruction.

In a marriage, when one or both partners change their beliefs, it puts incredible strain on the relationship.

I hate to say it, but my observation is most marriages don't survive it.

Marriage is about change. If you don't change as an individual, you aren't growing. If you don't change as a marriage, it's not growing either. We must learn how to constantly adapt to one another as we personally and relationally change and grow.

When Lisa and I went through a very intense period of deconstruction and left the ministry and the church, our marriage almost didn't survive.

It took determination to stay together until it started to make sense. It took patience waiting for clarity. It took figuring out why we fell in love in the first place. It took learning how to respect and appreciate the new her, me and "us". It took daring to communicate about our changes.

Some people realize they got married for the wrong reasons. They realize that their marriage wasn't good anyway. They realize they aren't in love and never will be. They split up and move on. That's okay.

But if you want to stay together and work it out, communication is key. You have to dare to rouse your courage and open your mouth and speak your mind, even if you don't know what to say.

Even if it's as simple as starting with: "I'm questioning my beliefs" or "I'm having doubts about my faith" or "I feel like I don't want to go to church anymore" or "I'm really confused about how to go forward in our relationship" or "... fill in the blank... "

Yes, it's going to be difficult and scary. But if you care about one another and talk, you will figure it out. We did. You can.

Just talk. No preparation. No script. Just talk.

And see what happens.

Homework:

Talk with your partner about how you feel your beliefs have changed and where you need space for that. Allow your partner the same. No interruptions.

MARRIED AND CHANGING YOUR BELIEFS

What if Lisa changes her beliefs? What will I do? What if I change mine? What will she do?

I remember when this happened with Lisa and me. It was a very sad and scary time. It lasted for a couple of years. I seriously wondered if we were going to survive it.

Many marriages don't. I know this because I talk with these people all the time. My online community, The Lasting Supper, has many people who struggle with their changing beliefs within a marriage. They need a safe place to talk about it. That's what we endeavor to provide.

My most important piece of advice I give to people who are going through this is just one thing: communicate! Talk about it! Communication is absolutely the most important ingredient to any relationship, but especially a relationship that is going through traumatic change.

Because when one of you changes, the other one has to as well. This is what love does. True love, healthy relationships, a good marriage, is like dancing through change.

But if you don't talk honestly, openly, vulnerably and authentically about everything, then it's much harder to navigate these rough waters.

Talk! Talk! Talk!

Look: I believe a healthy marriage means choosing one another over and over again, every single day. The person you are married to now is not exactly the same person you married years ago. They've changed. So have you. So you decide right from the start to choose to love the person in front of you from one day to the next.

And this takes conversation!

I know it's scary. It IS scary to say, "Will you love me if I change?" because it requires honesty, and honesty often comes with discomfort because our security is challenged.

But what I've discovered, is that talking about it has a greater return of success than not talking about it.

If you haven't learned how to communicate at this level of honesty, start now! Yes, it's hard. But if you want to save your marriage, it's worth it. Isn't it?

I know it has been worth it for Lisa and me. We are not identical spiritually like we used to be. We are very different. But we talk about it and love each other in our individuality and uniqueness now more than ever. Communication is worth it!

Homework:

What is one subject you and your partner haven't talked about and you know you need to?

YOU AND YOUR SPOUSE ON DIFFERENT SPIRITUAL PATHS

I see it happening all the time. And it makes me sad.

I've had so many couple friends split up because of the deconstruction of their beliefs... of one or both of them.

You already know my story. Lisa and I almost didn't make it. It took years to finally figure out how to love one another in fresh, new, and exciting ways.

There are three basic ingredients you need to get through it, if you want to.

1. Memory: Remember what drew you together, what attracted you to each other, and what you loved about each other. That's the essence of your relationship. For me, I'll be honest, I was first attracted to Lisa because she was the hottest girl on campus. Then, when I started to get to know her, I was attracted to her feistiness, her strong will and independence, her deep wisdom and her zest for life. Her beliefs weren't even on the list. Sure, we assumed a lot. But forty years later, Lisa still possesses those same essential attributes, including still being beautiful, and that's what makes her so desirable to me and contributes to our sturdy relationship. Always has. Figuring out our different beliefs is a game played upon this sturdy board. Just remember why you're even together in the first place!

2. Grace: Have grace for yourself and grace for your spouse. Don't judge. You're not watching a snapshot, you're watching a movie. You're observing the wonderful unfolding of an individual's life in remarkable ways... yours and your spouse's. Trust that they know what's best for themselves, just like you're trusting yourself to know what's best for you. The journey of explorers is never in a straight line, zigzagging all over the place, sometimes back, sometimes forward, but always towards the destination,

whatever that is… which you don't know until you get there. We are strange and wonderful human beings. Appreciate that! Be as gracious as you were with each other in your earliest days.

3. Patience: When deconstruction set in for Lisa and me, it was frightening. We had never ever navigated these waters before. They were strange, dangerous, and completely unpredictable. We had to paddle by the seat of our pants because not much had been written about this stuff before. No one told us, for example, that it was going to be a couple of years before we would start feeling stable or even in love again. There were times, literally, when bags were packed and we were heading our separate ways. I hate recalling those moments because we nearly ended a really good thing. I had friends advising me to just do what made me happy. I didn't trust myself, though. I was confused. So I made an important conclusion that I advise other people to follow too: Do NOT make a decision during confusing times. Wait for clarity! I'm so glad I did. Lisa and I waited for clarity. It took years, but it was so worth it. We're still together and better than we've ever been as a married couple. Get through this desert. There is an oasis on the other side of it. Promise. Be patient!

I always provide a disclaimer with this topic: Some marriages don't make it. Some people decide they were never meant to be married in the first place, or they realize that their marriage was never a good one to start with, or they decide there's just too much damage done to repair it. All these reasons and more are valid. I support people through these painful transitions as well. And I see many of them come through the other side of separation and divorce as happier and healthier people with a hopeful life ahead of them.

Memory, grace and patience. These will help your marriage survive deconstruction.

Homework:

What are some of your fondest memories together?

I AM QUESTIONING ALL MY BELIEFS, AND IT IS VERY DIFFICULT. BUT I WILL NEVER GIVE UP ON JESUS BECAUSE HE'S NEVER GIVEN UP ON ME!
©nakedpastor.com
POOF!

DECONSTRUCTION IS NOT BETRAYAL

I read about a person who said their spouse betrayed them because they questioned their beliefs. They made vows and their partner broke them. They felt they should have decided together if this was the right thing to do or not.

But you can't plan deconstruction (questioning your beliefs, losing your faith, and leaving the church). It's something that happens to you.

You don't wake up one morning and make a calculated decision: I'll question everything I've ever believed. I'll embark on the most traumatic spiritual crisis of my life. I'll stop going to church with my friends. I'll terrify my partner and destroy our marriage.

Deconstruction stalks you like a wolf: it takes a while but the attack is sudden.

I speak with many people. It's the most prevalent problem with married or attached believers who deconstruct. The trauma to the relationship is sudden, shocking, and sad. Your relationship as you knew it is gone.

This is one of the roughest patches your relationship will go through. But if you persevere you will prevail! I promise.

Your partner being true to themselves is not a betrayal of you.

I've experienced it and observed it. Here's my advice:

1. The one you fell in love with is still there. They're becoming a better person.
2. Remember: you fell in love with the person, not their theology.
3. Communicate, even when you are confused and it hurts. Try to talk.

4. Know that relationships can survive anything.
5. Respect one another's journeys. Theirs is theirs. Yours is yours.
6. Discover new ways to connect on a deep level.
7. Touch! Hold hands. Hug. Kiss. Make love. Your body can help your spirit.

You will make it!

Homework:

Do you feel betrayed by your partner? Talk about it. Maybe you might learn something different.

"WELL, WHICH ONE SHALL WE GO TO TODAY?"

WHEN YOU BREAK YOUR PARTNER'S HEART

Breaking hearts is a fine Christian tradition. In fact, I think the core message, that finds its roots firmly in the Old Testament and sprawling into the New, is the necessity to challenge the status quo and press into what's true, no matter the consequences for our relationships.

Some might argue that if someone's heart breaks, it's that person's own responsibility, not the heart-breaker's. But I would challenge that. I think it is a symbiotic occurrence. This is what happens when people change. It stretches the relationship, sometimes to the extreme, and forces those around the person determined to be true to change. All relationships are like a crucible into which all parties enter and from which no party remains unscathed or unchanged.

But... what if a party refuses to change? This is when a divorce in the relationship happens.

Unfortunately, I think a lot of Christianity today nourishes the status quo and tends to excommunicate those who refuse to cooperate. The story of Jesus is a case in point. Whether you believe the story is factual or not, the story itself demonstrates the risks and costs of challenging authorized norms.

Undergoing personal transformation, challenging the status quo and paying dearly for it, is a richly cultivated theme of the Jesus story.

It's in Christianity's blood!

Homework:

How are you being stretched by your partner? Are you willing to go through this process? How are you stretching your partner? Are they on board?

YOUR WHOLE LIFE DOESN'T HAVE TO FALL APART

When I left the church in 2010 I was numb for about a year. I thought I was doing awesome when in fact I was completely unaware of how unwell I really was.

I was going through a massive transition and my favorite way of dealing with stress is to turn off self-awareness and wait till it's over. Then, when it's passed, I evaluate it and try to integrate it. Often, it's too late.

When it dawned on me that I was unemployed, that we were financially bankrupt, that our kids had left home, leaving us with an empty nest, that we'd lost almost all of our friends, that my marriage was in trouble… that's when I realized I needed help.

Changing your religious habits and beliefs is traumatic. Deconstruction involves demolition, and that's never nice. Necessary, but not nice. I've never seen it otherwise. It's like everything gets tossed up into the wind, like wheat and chaff.

So I encourage you to be aware of this. Work on what you can work on. Keep what you can keep. Let the rest go.

Even though your beliefs are falling apart, it doesn't mean your finances, your home, your marriage or your life have to too.

Homework:

What in your relationship MUST be dealt with? What can wait?

HOW TO CHANGE IN FRONT OF YOUR KIDS

Someone who liked my cartoon yesterday, love trumps belief: when your partner believes differently, asked about how to do this with children. I promised to do that today. This is a letter I wrote for the members of The Lasting Supper last year. I hope you find it helpful.

Here's the letter (slightly edited):

I'd been looking forward to working on this letter and sending it to you today. Many people have been asking me to write about this issue. Obviously it is an important one that occupies many of our minds and evokes concern in our hearts.

It's about our children. How do we deconstruct with our kids?

(***NOTE: This doesn't just apply to our kids. You can apply these principles to any loved one... a partner, a family member or a friend. One thing I've learned: The way you do one thing is the way you do everything. The way you treat anybody is the way you treat everybody.)

I'm going to talk about how to deconstruct with your children. As parents we like to appear that we are in control of our lives and by inference the lives of our kids. We like to be responsible. So when we experience the death-throes of the deconstruction of our faith and beliefs and experience confusion, how do we take care of the spiritual lives of our own children? How do we oversee the spiritual development of our kids when we can't even oversee our own?

Here are a few suggestions that are more about themes than advice.

1. Relinquish Control But Not Responsibility:

Many people grow up in very tightly controlled homes where their spirituality is assigned. When I became a father I wanted to do it differently and help my children find their own selves and their own paths. We relinquished control. At the same time, we saw ourselves as gentle guides... like spiritual sherpas... showing our kids where the possible pitfalls and the safest pathways were, what foods were good and what wasn't, and who and what to trust or not.

When Lisa and I left the church our children were already in their older teens, so they were already well on their way. We could hold adult conversations with mature themes. When Lisa and I were talking about this topic the other day, she said our kids were already deconstructing before we were because we allowed them to question from an early age. They had the ability, without our baggage, to be honest about what was real, authentic and true and the strength to reject what didn't pass that test. They were far more sensitive to control and nonsense than we were because they were raised differently than we were. So when we started deconstructing, they were already prepped for it.

We had obviously raised our kids in the Christian faith. We still have a collection of children's bible story books that we used read from them every night. They grew up in the church, so they knew the stories, the traditions and what church means. But we never required them to believe this or that. Like the sower with the seeds, we cast the seeds everywhere, knowing that what was good would stick and what wasn't wouldn't because it depended on what kind of soil their own hearts were. They'd develop their own spirituality and therefore find the special food that needed to feed it.

In 2002 Lisa's father had come to live with us because he was dying of cancer. This was when we were in New Hampshire, planting a church for a ministry. The day before Christmas, Lisa's father died. Our approach to it was to try to understand it theologically, and we had our long-held world-views and the ministry people to bolster this attempt. Not our kids! They loved their papa, and when they watched him die in our house despite all the prayers and promises, they immediately questioned what all those prayers and promises claimed to be. So they not only questioned that, but they went to the source: God! They realized that the idea of God everyone talked about and what actually is are completely different things. The ministry fired me the next day, and the church I planted and all the staff ignored us. We never saw them again. This, for my kids, was inexcusable. So they saw the church for what it was: just another collection of disappointing human beings. Not to say that they don't think people and our groups can't be good, but that the church has no divine right to claim that it is good by default. If you say you're good, you have to walk the talk.

So we continued relinquishing control but kept our responsibility by allowing them to process this trauma in their own way. When our kids, who were very attached to papa, cried, "I don't believe in God anymore!" we didn't try to correct or balance them or even affirm their developing belief. We just let them say it and deal with it in their own way. As a result, years later, they have their own spirituality that is uniquely theirs. It isn't the same as ours, and this is as it ought to be. We saw that they required a spirituality free of smoke and mirrors, magical thinking, and horse-and-pony shows.

2. Acknowledge Their Intellectual Curiosity and Honesty Without Surrendering Yours:

When our children asked hard questions we found it very tempting to give easy answers. Sometimes we're just too exhausted to explain everything. Sometimes we're just too confused. Sometimes we're afraid and just want them to believe the magical thinking that religion is so good at nurturing. Sometimes we just couldn't care.

Lisa and I sometimes fought. We decided when they were young that we wouldn't pretend that our marriage was out of Disney but the struggling union of two real, flesh and blood people. Lisa and I have been married 35 years. So our kids have seen us fight. Our strategy was to let them see us argue but also let them see us resolve it. If I offended Lisa and the kids saw it, we would also let them watch me apologize and see us reconcile (yes, it was honestly usually my fault).

So when we went through our own deconstructions, we let our kids watch. When our kids questioned the existence of the rescuing God that our Christianity promoted, this affected us. We didn't interpret it as a rebellion, backsliding or foolishness. We recognized the fear that their questions invoked in us. It's terrible to think your children are forsaking your path and taking their own instead. But we had to believe that they, like us, would find their way. We would continue to point out dangers and make suggestions, but primarily we trusted that if their intelligence had integrity, they would make it.

As David Schnarch says in his book, Passionate Marriage: Keeping Love and Intimacy Alive in Committed Relationships, relationships are formed and transformed in a crucible. When one person changes, it forces the other to change. Otherwise the relationship will fail. It's the same with the relationship with our kids. If they change, it forces us to change. If we change, it forces them to change. It's a perpetual dance. So when our kids changed direction theologically, we had to in some ways go their way while at the same time not forsaking our own. When we changed, if they wanted to remain in relationship with us, they had to adjust their steps as well without forsaking their integrity. Unlike the homes many people grow up in, it wasn't "My way or the highway!" It was an intersection of our own highways weaving in and out of each other. As a result, we hopefully fostered a respect for their journeys and in them a respect for ours. That still holds.

3. Respect Their Discoveries and Conclusions But Allow For Cross-Pollination:

Our children formed opinions that differed from ours. So in our house there was the fascinating interplay of five different opinions. This isn't to say that the five world views blended together to become one syncretistic stew called Haywardism. Instead, our different beliefs were uniquely our own in a home that fostered a mutual respect for the other. And when I say different, this could even mean contradictory. It is like a United Nations of Spirituality. But Lisa and I learned early in our relationship that it wasn't compatibility of beliefs that held us together. It was a love that respected the other no matter where they were. Lisa and I believe very differently, but we love each other. That's the glue that binds us.

There have been difficult times when our differences created sparks that could have possibly turned into a raging fire that might have incinerated us. But I guess we learned how to negotiate those heated moments in ways that enabled us to put the fire out, divert it, or let it burn off the dross and change us.

Without a doubt, our kids learned from us. Without a doubt, we learned from them. Perhaps our kids learned from us how to be persistent, steadfast and faithful through difficult times. Perhaps we learned from our kids how to be honest, independent and outspoken through times of pressure to conform. While we taught our kids to think for themselves and believe what they believe with integrity, they also forced us to do the same. We've told them our version. They've told us theirs. We've told them our stories. They've told us theirs. We pollinated them. They pollinated us. Like a hardy apple that has developed over the years through cross-pollination, we have fed off each other and developed traits that hopefully help us to survive even in the harshest of conditions.

Conclusion:

I don't want to give the impression that we are a perfect family. We are not perfect! We have our issues and problems as individuals and collectively. But there is a love and mutual respect that keeps us together. There have been moments and seasons of unbelievable stress and confusion. There have been terrors and tensions. There have been separations and reconciliations. But so far we have survived them.

I was tempted at first to give maybe a 10 point list of advice for parents going through deconstruction in front of their kids... things like let them see the books you read and answer their curiosities about them; teach your kids how to think, not how to believe; tell them everything you're going through and let them deal with what it means for them; ask them what they believe and listen objectively and engage in conversation about it; openly share your struggles with what you're going through with the church and let them process it themselves, and so on. Rather, I thought I would give the three points above as sturdy blocks that help build an authentic, honest and thoughtful life.

Homework:

Have you and your partner sat down with your kids to discuss the obvious changes your relationship is going through in a way they can understand and appreciate?

I FEEL LIKE WE DIED THERE. DO YOU THINK WE WILL EVER FEEL ALIVE AGAIN?

STEPS TO MAKING NEW FRIENDS FOR YOUR MARRIAGE

As many of you know, one of the worst aspects of leaving the church is losing all or most of your friends, and the difficulty of making new ones.

We may experience extreme loneliness after we leave the church, and some of us fall into the rut of accepting that loneliness as our way of life from now on and forsake the idea of having good friends ever again.

Especially when our marriage is under strain and the same intimacy we used to enjoy is missing, loneliness can become a very real issue.

Lisa and I experienced exactly this after we left the church in 2010. We did lose almost all of our friends, kept only a few and experienced long stretches of loneliness.

But now, some years later, we have a pretty healthy list of friends. We would like to see it grow and develop, but essentially we do not experience extended periods of loneliness like we used to. Usually, if we have the time and want to see friends, it happens. Cool!

How did we do it? Because it has to be done. It has to be intentional. We discovered pretty quickly that if we just waited for it to happen, it wouldn't. We came to realize that almost everyone is dealing with the very same issue.

So here's a list of things Lisa and I did that I suggest you try in order to make new friends. I've even included some copy-and-paste texts for you to use if you want.

1. Don't take it personally. If someone doesn't pursue you like you are pursuing them, we found out that most often they are too busy, too afraid, or too shy to initiate. If they refuse three times in a row without a good reason, let them go. It's supposed to be fun, not laborious. "We're trying hard to see you guys. Can we

make it happen this week?"

2. Schedule it in. If you don't schedule time to get together with others, your schedule won't allow it. Life is crazy busy for everyone I know. Live life. Don't let it live you! Make it happen. "What are you guys doing Saturday morning? Want to meet us for brunch?"

3. Restore old friends. Are there people you used to be friends with that you've lost touch with? We restored a few older friendships and it was worth it. "Hey, for some reason we've been thinking about you guys and were wondering if you'd like to get together.

4. Pick up clues. If someone you work with or run into often or whatever hints about getting together, take it seriously. Take them up on it! "You mentioned us getting together last week. Shall we? We're pretty free this weekend!"

5. Choose a neutral place. Lisa and I often prefer to go out than have people in. With us both working hard, it's just easier because we don't have to clean the house immaculately, prepare food, or take the risk of people staying far later than our bedtime. Plus, it's just nice eating out. It's something we enjoy. "Hey! We're going out to Italian-by-Night and want to know if you'd like to meet us there. Say, 7pm?"

6. Extend invitations. One night at a pub with friends, we met friends of theirs. They seemed cool. They'd heard about nakedpastor. We talked. Next time we see them we just might say something like, "We enjoyed meeting you guys that night. We should meet there again sometime. Ya?"

7. Keep it up. Don't relax your efforts. Making friends, we found out, is hard work. And, just like any relationship (including marriage) it takes hard work to maintain. Contact friends every week. "Hi guys! We haven't seen you in a while. What's up? Can we get together this week?"

8. Detoxify. If you have friends you discover are toxic, as in they don't accept you as you are and are a drain on your wellbeing… like they are trying to get you saved, trying to get you to go to their church, trying to burden you with their problems, trying

to make your life miserable and negative. Just let them go. Feel no guilt over ending a relationship. Do not carry over from your church days the idea that we must always forgive and reconcile with every single person who's ever been in our life no matter how bad they are for us. End toxic relationships! For this one there is no text. Just stop cold turkey.

9. Go to events. Art gallery hops, wine tastings, Toast Masters, join a choir, go to staff parties... anything! Get out where people are. If you used to go to church, you know these events were provided for you. Now you have to seek them out yourself. Meet new people. Follow up on any leads. Lisa and I went to an event once, and we were hanging out with people there. As the evening progressed, a few said, "We're gong to such-and-such a bar after. Wanna come?" Take those opportunities.

10. Appreciate the few. I've known a lot of people over the years. Most people just have a few good friends, then maybe a wider group of just friends or acquaintances. This is normal, folks! When a friendship feels really good, develop it. Work on it. You could become very good friends.

Also, enjoy the just friends friends too. "Hi! We really enjoyed the other night with you guys. We should get together more often." Chances are they are wishing for good friends too.

I hope this helps. Remember, friends hardly ever just happen. They take work. They take noticing clues. They take follow up. They take development. They take intentionality. They take commitment.

You don't have to go through the rest of your life lonely. You don't have to long for the good old days when you had a whole raft of friends handed to you on a platter because of high school or church. You can enjoy friendships now.

Happy friending!

Homework:

Together, write out a short list of people you would like to have as good friends. Contact them. Initiate conversations. Make plans. Start today!

SO WHEN YOU SAY YOU WANT TO LEAVE EVERYTHING THAT BURDENS YOU WITH EXPECTATIONS AND HOLDS YOU BACK FROM BEING YOUR TRUE SELF, YOU ARE TALKING ABOUT THE CHURCH, RIGHT?
AND YOU.
Hayward
©nakedpastor.com

WHEN YOUR MARRIAGE DOESN'T SURVIVE DECONSTRUCTION

This post is sad but it's real.

When deconstruction strikes a marriage it can be devastating.

By "deconstruction", we mean the changing of belief, the loss of faith, or leaving the church.

By "strikes a marriage", I mean when one or both partners experience deconstruction.

In my observation, many marriages don't survive.

There are several reasons why:

1. They realize the only reason they got married was to have sex purely and legally. They wanted to have sex, but the only way was to get married. Now, years later and starting to question everything about the faith and the church, they admit getting married just to have sex isn't a good enough reason to stay together. Especially if sex is no longer an important part of the relationship.

2. They discover that they're not really in love. They pretended they were because of pressure from the church to behave as though they were. It takes a lot of self-awareness and honesty to say, "You know what? I don't love him/her. I never really did!" Once they admit that, then they realize there's no reason to keep trying to make this work.

3. They conclude that since they have changed so much and that they no longer feel compatible, it's not worth the effort required to fix it. "They are not the person I married, and I don't have the energy or the time to try to fall in love with this version of them!" They feel so out of sync with each other that the happiness is gone and there's no point in continuing.

4. They want to abandon anything to do with their religious past, including their spouse. I'll be honest with you: this was one that nearly broke up my marriage. I wanted to run from everything. I escaped religion and the church, abhorred the thought of feeling trapped, and considered walking away from everything, including my wife. It was a confusing time. Some don't survive this impulse and do leave everything associated with their past, including their marriage.

5. They decide that they were married too young and have never known anything but married life, have never colored outside the lines, and were never allowed to live authentically without being responsible to or for another. Related to this are people who discover they're not monogamous or heterosexual or their assigned gender, etcetera. Many go their separate ways in order to live their own way... something they've never done before.

A huge part of the problem is the stigma of divorce that survives in our minds from our religious days. You remember: God hates divorce and you should suffer long even in a terrible marriage because that's always better than divorce. But I do not judge anyone going through this or for the decision they make. It's always messy. It's never clean. I've said it before, if you can make your marriage work because you want to, then work hard to do it. But if you want to end it, do it as well as you can. The goal is the personal wellbeing of each person and taking the steps necessary to make sure that happens.

If divorce seems to be the only viable option, I recommend that you still get counseling. It's a difficult process, and having a wise counselor guide you through it is worth every penny. It is possible for your divorce to be an amicable one. Especially if there are children involved.

Perhaps you can add other reasons marriages don't survive deconstruction.

Homework:

What is one thing you can do to preserve some good from your relationship? What value do you want to take from your marriage?

GET HELP FOR YOUR MARRIAGE

Although this is short and sweet, deconstruction is not.

My argument is simple:

Get help!

What I mean is: use whatever resources are available to you to invest in your own personal growth.

When I got last year's taxes done, I saw in black and white (and red) exactly how much I invested in my businesses. I also saw exactly how much I spent on myself and my own personal growth.

I paid thousands of dollars for therapy, counseling, spiritual direction, and coaching. That's beside all the help I got incidentally for free or from bartering.

I do this because I realized long ago that, just like the growth of my business is proportionate to how much I invest in it, so it is with me. The more I invest in my own personal growth, the more I personally grow!

Plus, I did this all while trying to undo the decades of negative and limiting beliefs I was fed and consumed surrounding money. In fact, that has been a large part of my personal growth.

It amazes me that people won't think twice about repairing their car when it breaks down, but to pay for help in their personal lives is offensive to them.

Unfortunately, many of them stay in a state of disrepair. I've seen marriages break up forever just because the guy's pride refuses to pay for a marriage counselor. He'd rather lose the love of his life than admit he needs help and lay the money down.

Right now I'm in a coaching group and learning the ropes on starting my own coaching business. It's expensive, but it's worth it. It's making me a better person and will help make me a better coach.

So get help! And pay for it! You'll be glad you did.

Homework:

Look online or ask around to find a good local relationship counselor and make that phone call to ask about availability and cost.

These people love each other. That means they trust one another with their own spiritual journeys.

QUESTION: WHICH COUPLE IS 'UNEQUALLY YOKED'?

THE ONE THING THAT WILL KILL A MARRIAGE

One of the areas of our life most affected when we go through major spiritual change is our relationships.

Fellow-workers, employers, family, friends, and even enemies.

Significant others, partners or spouses.

So this chapter is about our romantic relationships or marriages.

I've shared this with you before, but one of the most precious things I nearly lost during my time of deconstruction, changing my theology, leaving the ministry and the church, was my marriage to Lisa. We have made it and are better now than ever. But if we didn't have some marriage knowledge and tools, we might not have survived the traumatic shifts we were experiencing.

(*** disclaimer: This isn't to say that I believe all marriages should stick together. Sometimes separation and divorce is the healthiest thing for one or both of the partners. I just wanted to put that out there that I don't assume because you are married that you should always be or that if you have experienced divorce that somehow you failed.)

One of the books I've always fallen back on and always recommend for marriages is David Schnark's Passionate Marriage.

I'm glad I have that book and had read it.

But there's more!

Some years ago, after reading about it in Malcolm Gladwell's book Blink, I read John Gottman's book The Seven Principals for Making Marriage Work.

Even though he gives seven principals, he says there is one major one that makes or breaks a relationship.

Gottman can listen to a couple for 5 minutes and determine with 91% accuracy whether the couple will divorce or not.

Do you want to know what the key ingredient is?

First, let me tell you about Gottman's "Four Horsemen" that will split up a marriage. They are:

1. Criticism: where you attack the person, not just their behavior.
2. Contempt: name-calling, eye-rolling, sneering, mockery and hostile humor.
3. Defensiveness: blaming the other for all the problems.
4. Stonewalling: where you disengage, stall, deny, or ignore problems.

But the one thing that will split up a marriage faster than anything is #2, contempt. If Gottman detects this in the first five minutes of a session with a married couple, that helps him determine if they're going to make it or not. If one of the partners conveys disgust about their spouse, it is virtually impossible to resolve any problems. This, he claims, is the deadliest poison to a marriage.

I believe he's right. I've seen it myself after years of giving marriage counseling!

The fact is, this is the deadliest poison to any relationship. I see it online all the time. Many times every day. If someone expresses disdain, disgust or contempt for another person, it is absolutely impossible to have a mature and fruitful conversation. It's just not going to happen. The truth is, it pollutes the whole thread and turns everybody off until everyone eventually leaves. I witness this far too often.

One of the most difficult things to do in a marriage relationship is to allow the other to grow at his or her own pace while they let you grow at yours. When Lisa and I were in the ministry and in the church, we were pretty much on the same page. In 2010, after I had my waterfalls dream and started developing what I temporarily call "The Z-Theory", plus started experiencing difficulties staying in the ministry, we could feel the bonds between us starting to stretch.

It got to the point where we sometimes felt we were not only no longer on the same page, but no longer in the same book.

But time... four or five years in fact... has taught us that indeed we were in the same story. Ours! Our different spiritual journeys have shown us that we can grow together not only in depth but in breadth as well. We have widened the skirts of our tent and assumed even more under our roof.

Our relationship, our marriage, is richer for it.

Fortunately, we avoided the biggest pitfall... contempt. Somehow we maintained our mutual respect for one another, even though we may have been completely mystified by and irritated with one another at times.

I entrusted her to her own journey. She entrusted me to mine. We trusted that we would eventually feel like we were sharing the same story.

It worked.

So I guess you need to ask yourself:

- "Do I have contempt for my spouse?"
- "Does he or she have contempt for me?"
- "What am I going to do about it?"

Homework:

Have you gotten to the point where you hold contempt for you partner? Discuss.

I hope you don't mind me saying that I can see the spirit of Jesus in you.
If you don't mind me saying that I can see the Buddha nature in you.
©nakedpastor.com

STAYING IN LOVE WHEN YOU DON'T BELIEVE THE SAME

This takes seconds to see but can take years in real life.

This is Lisa's and my story.

When deconstruction hit our marriage (changing beliefs, losing faith as we knew it, and quitting church), it was devastating. We didn't know how to be together. We didn't even know how to talk. The glue we assumed held us together (a mixture of being on the same page of belief, being in ministry together, and being a part of a community of believers) disintegrated.

We had to figure out, if we wanted our marriage to survive, how to stay together. What was the real glue of our relationship that had lasted 30 years so far?

We recalled what initially attracted us to one another. For me, it was Lisa's looks. Her body. Her eyes. Her face. Her hair. Then her demeanor. Then I appreciated her personality... wild, uncontrollable, strong, independent, and wise. Never once was I enamored by her beliefs.

Of course, we were willingly immersed in a super religious culture at a Pentecostal Bible College. But I realized that if I was an animal in a conservation, a compound, or a cage, these environments won't matter when I'm attracted to another.

We realized that love is the glue. Not compatibility!

Ask, if you're in a relationship experiencing deconstruction:

What initially attracted us to one another?

Can we get in touch with that again?

Is my original lover still in there somewhere?

Does my partner's choices make sense within the total picture of their personality?

Can I respect them for the journey they've embarked upon?

Will I be afforded the same grace for my spiritual choices?

You can make it! We did.

Homework:

What about your partner do you find really attractive right now?

WHEN WE HIRED YOU AS OUR PASTOR, WE ASSUMED YOU'D KEEP YOUR WIFE IN LINE!
@nakedpastor.com

DECONSTRUCTING SPOUSES OF MINISTRY SPOUSES

Deconstruction is the change of beliefs, the loss of faith, leaving the church, or all three.

It's one thing when a couple goes through deconstruction.

It's another when one goes through deconstruction before or instead of the other.

It's still another when the spouse of a church leader goes through deconstruction.

I mostly say "wife" in this post because I speak with mostly women who are deconstructing ahead of or in spite of their ministry husbands, rather than the other way around. But it does happen.

So, this is about wives whose deconstruction threatens their husbands' ministry.

When the wife of a church leader changes her beliefs, it threatens the stability of the consistent and growing ministry the congregation expects.

When things start falling apart, the wife is accused of backsliding, dishonoring her husband, destroying her family, betraying the church, and denying Christ.

If this is you, this is how I encourage you:

1. Count the Cost: Anyone who deconstructs experiences risk. You too should estimate what the damage will be martially, socially, and financially. Then determine how and how fast to proceed.

2. Keep Growing: I was a pastor but left because of my deconstruction. Either that or stop growing! Your personal growth is most important and necessary. It's your choice how you navigate it.

3. Find Company: Be relieved that you're not crazy, that your spiritual growth is healthy, and that you're not alone. There are many wives going through the same thing!

4. Believe in Yourself: I'm impressed by your integrity, strength, and courage. Many shrink back, justifiably afraid of upheaval, ridicule, and rejection. But you are determined to be your authentic self in spite of the cost.

Once you see that you are amazing, nothing can stop you.

Homework:

Has your deconstruction or your spouses or both affected your participation or role in the church? How? Can this continue? Or is this going to radically change how you function in the church if you stay?

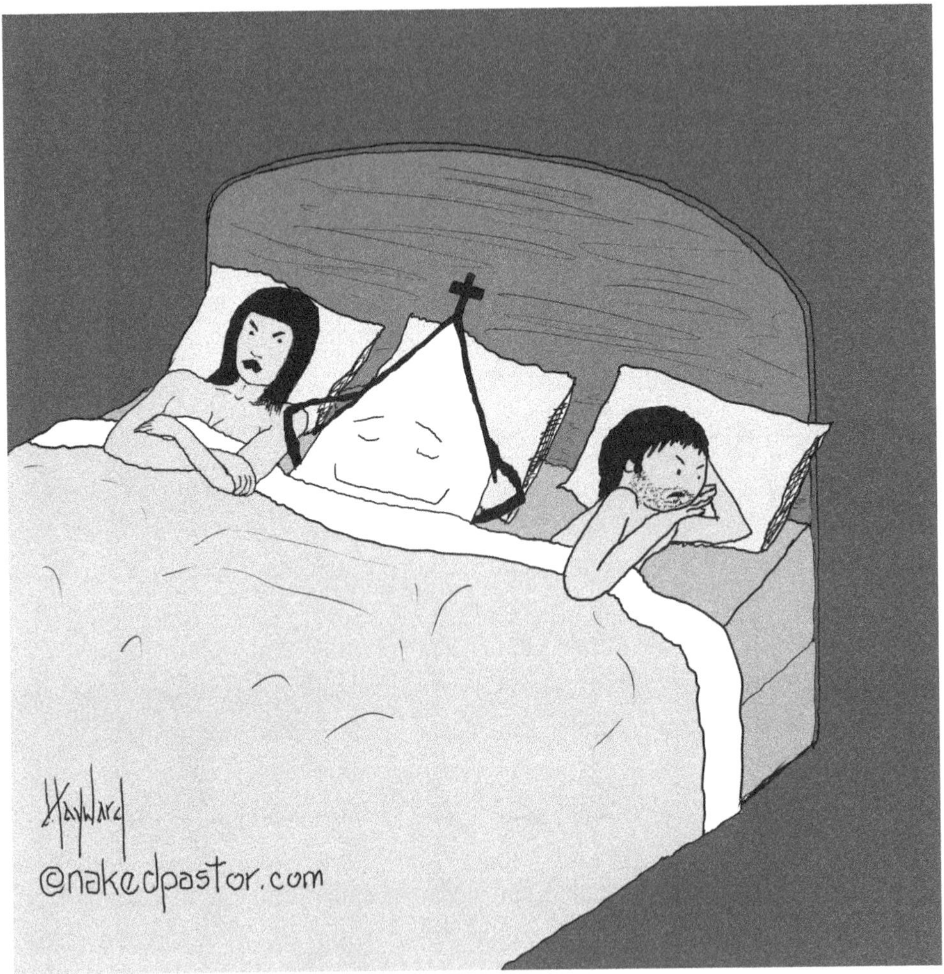
Hayward
©nakedpastor.com

HAS THE CHURCH COME BETWEEN YOU?

Lisa and I met in the church, got married in the church, raised our family in the church, then later on left the church.

We came to realize that it wasn't the church and our beliefs that should hold us together, but our love for one another.

We'd come to a place where the church was getting in the way of our growth... personally and relationally.

It was time to become spiritually independent.

That was a hard transition to make.

But we made it, and you can too!

Homework:

List the ways you feel the church has interfered in your relationship. Are there ways you can create healthy boundaries? List those too.

Well THAT'S a first...
making love to a streaming
church service!
@nakedpastor.com

Marriage, Deconstruction, and Having Fun

I call this cartoon "Streaming or Steamy Church"

Changing your beliefs changes your relationships.

Change and others must adapt if they want to stay in relationship with you.

Same for marriage! If you change, your partner must change. If your partner changes, then you must change. We learn to adapt to the other, give them room to grow, and provide a safe space for their transformation to unfold.

But it's important to have fun along the way.

Lisa and I found that as we grew and changed it made it easier and happier if we could be lighthearted and even make fun of ourselves.

Laughter's good medicine.

This doesn't mean we despise, ridicule, or shame our earlier lives. Rather, we hold our former selves with compassion as part of our story. We would not be who we are now if we hadn't been who we were then. The fact that we can look back with gentleness on where we were and how we got here is affirming, liberating and joyful.

Lisa was 19 and I was 22 when we got married. What did we know?! In our youthful Pentecostal naïveté we wrestled with sexual and relational questions that are immaterial now. Even though we enjoyed each other, we were far too serious in our ardor for what was righteous. We had some self-liberating to do!

So, we laugh!

All beliefs must be falsifiable if they are to be taken seriously. Armed with this attitude, we can enjoy them as they are: provisional attempts to apprehend and articulate the deepest mysteries of an abundant and joyful life!

This is an adventure almost as exciting as exploring one another's bodies.

Homework:

What used to make you laugh together? What makes you laugh now? When was the last time you laughed together? What was it about?

LOVING RELATIONSHIPS AND CHANGING BELIEFS

If you are one of the people in this cartoon, I have a warning and some good news.

It's very scary when the person you love changes.

The person you've always loved has always been a certain way. Now they're not. They seem to be transforming into someone else! Maybe someone you didn't sign up for.

I think premarital counseling must include warnings that the person you love right now, sitting right here in front of you, that you are absolutely head over heels over, is going to change.

This includes their beliefs. Your partner may one day not be the steadfast believer you know, love, and respect today.

Lisa and I have been married for 40-plus years. Our beliefs have changed so dramatically that back then we wouldn't have recognized ourselves as we are now.

But here's the good news: we're not just different, we're better!

Why?

Because we've grown. We've developed. We're more independent and authentic. We're more ourselves than ever before. We are evolving into who we really are. We've courageously stepped up to personal growth and are developing our relationship skills.

It's like a blossoming! Yes, we've changed. But we've also burst open and we and our relationship are more beautiful than ever.

Yes, it can be sad, shocking, and grievous to say goodbye to the former selves.

But it can be exciting to say hello to the newer selves.

When we say "I do promise to love this person", you're not just saying it to the person you see in front of you now, but to the person they will fully become that you haven't even had a glimpse of yet.

Buckle up for more!

10 BOOKS FOR COMMITTED ROMANTIC RELATIONSHIPS

Because some of our members have requested this, I am listing 10 of the most helpful books I could find in my library about committed relationships. I'm sure there must be some missing that we've loaned out. But here's what I got.

(Now, I want to assert that the best way to make a good relationship is to be healthy yourself. This is always the first step. Take care of yourself and you've mastered the work. Because, let's admit it, you're not going to change our partner. That's their job!)

So here are some books that Lisa and I count among the most influential in helping us:

1. David Schnarch, Passionate Marriage: Keeping Love and Intimacy Alive in Committed Relationships. (A must! This outshines them all. If I could only recommend one book, this would be it! From communication to sex. #1 on Amazon for this topic.)

2. Melody Beattie, Codependent No More: How to Stop Controlling Others and Start Caring for Yourself. (This is a powerful book that applies to all relationships but is also helpful for marriage. This caused a turning point in our marriage.)

3. Daniel Coleman, Emotional Intelligence. (A great book that helps people realize the importance of expressing emotions with guides on how to do it.)

4. Psaris and Lyons, Undefended Love: The Way That You Felt When You First Fell in Love is the Way You Can Feel All the Time. (Dropping our defenses is the best way to open ourselves up to the love of another.)

5. Don Miguel Ruiz, The Mastery of Love: A Practical Guide to the Art of Relationship. (He wrote "The Four Agreements". Just plain

simple wisdom for healthy love.)

6. Adele Faber and Elaine Mazlish, How To Talk So Kids Will Listen and Listen so Kids Will Talk. (Although we read this tiny paperback to help us raise our kids well, it actually taught Lisa and me how to communicate with each other in healthy, non-aggressive and respectful ways.)

7. Sandra D. Wilson, Shame-Free Parenting. (Her tagline is "Are you trying to love your children a lot when you don't like yourself even a little?" That, in my opinion, counts for our partners as well.)

8. David Keirsey and Marilyn Bates, Please Understand Me: Character and Temperament Types. (One of the best ways to make a better relationship is to understand and appreciate the uniqueness of the other. There's a short test at the end of the book to help you discover your personality type that is fun to do together. Eye-opening and revelatory! It even has a section that will describe your relationship based on your personality types.)

9. Edward M. Hallowell and Sue George Hallowell, Married to Distraction: Restoring Intimacy and Strengthening Your Marriage in an Age of Interruption. (No joke: Lisa's read this book and says I need to but I've been too busy. She says it's awesome and a must. I will. I promise. Soon. It says it's for "those hungry to move beyond conflict and condemnation to connection and understanding.")

10. What's your suggestion? Anyone?

Homework:

READ SOME OF THESE BOOKS! They contain help!

CONCLUSION

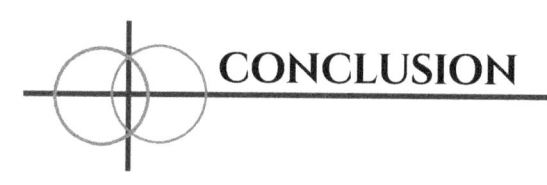

I really hope this book and course has helped you... helped you to save your marriage or to go your separate ways amicably.

If you want to contact me for coaching related to this topic, please email me at haywardart@gmail.com

Peace on your path and love in your life!

David Hayward

CPSIA information can be obtained
at www.ICGtesting.com
Printed in the USA
LVHW091651040221
678381LV00029B/707

9 798663 893749